Mary

Sew Powerful Parables

Written by
DANA BUCK

Illustrated by
SHONDA BOWDEN

SEW POWERFUL PUBLISHING 2019

Audio versions of Sew Powerful Parables are available at
www.sewpowerful.org/parables

Sew Powerful Media
Sew Powerful Parables
By Dana Buck

Published in the United States by Sew Powerful Media

Sew Powerful Media
218 E. Main Street
Auburn WA 98092

ISBN- 9781793825902

Library Of Congress Numbers:

The Pandaroo -	TXu 2-029-188
You Do Your Part, I'll do Mine	TXu 2-033-256
Steve the Sheep	TXu 2-029-122
Flawless	TXu 2-014-349
An American Parable	TXu 2-013-905
A Dog Named Tongue	TXu 2-062-952
Gabriella's Shoes	TXu 2-018-321
Honest Henry's Store	TXu 2-024-411
Earl the Lonely Beaver	TXu 2-014-134
The Rule of Thumb	TXu 2-038-445
Pepper the Prodigal Cat	TXu 2-037-746

Printed by CreateSpace, a DBA of On-Demand Publishing, LLC

⇒ TABLE of CONTENTS ⇐

FOREWORD

God's Word never gets old. It doesn't matter how many times we read the Bible, hear a sermon, or retell beloved Sunday school stories – again and again, we glean fresh insights and meaningful life lessons.

Prepare yourself for both when you read this book by my friend Dana Buck. Fair warning: it's probably unlike any Bible story collection you've ever read. Part Dr. Seuss, part Eugene Peterson, *Sew Powerful Parables* is a treasure.

I've known Dana for 20 years. We were colleagues at World Vision U.S., where he served for more than 38 years before recently retiring. Humble, upbeat, fun-loving, and godly, Dana was an ebullient presence around the office, a true "people person" who made everyone feel like his best friend. Outside of work he was deeply involved with his church as a longtime youth mentor and mission trip leader.

A few years ago, Dana discovered a remarkable gift for writing. Once he got started, the stories poured out of him, written in witty, imaginative verse and revealing profound ideas about God. Word got around at World Vision about Dana's "parables," as he called them, and he became a frequent speaker at department devotions and chapel services. We couldn't get enough of Dana's stories and the truths they imparted. I encouraged him to publish them so that they could be shared more widely, and I'm thrilled that he has done just that.

Sew Powerful Parables are whimsical tales set in both modern-day and biblical times, featuring plotlines that will amuse you and characters you'll find relatable. Some stories humanize biblical figures like Noah and his sons, bringing their struggles to life. Others use animals and even an egotistical thumb to creatively interpret familiar Scripture passages. The clever rhymes are easy to read aloud, making this a great choice for family devotions or with ministry groups (for inspiration, you can listen to Dana read them himself at sewpowerful.org).

But like the best storytelling, they go deep. They illuminate biblical values such as forgiveness, generosity, obedience, and, of course, God's great love for us. That's what the Bible is, after all: the story of a Father's love for his children.

My prayer is that everyone who reads these parables will feel even more intimately a part God's big story – a world-changing mission of love and compassion. All the ordinary people (and animals) Dana writes about are just like us, struggling to find our place and purpose in a fallen world. What makes all our stories *so powerful* is when we discover who we are in Christ and what we've been created to do. And that's a tale worth telling again and again.

—**Richard Stearns**, World Vision U.S. President Emeritus and the author of *The Hole in Our Gospel* and *Unfinished*

THE PANDAROO

When you feel like you don't fit in

For you created my inmost being; you knit me together in my mother's womb. I praise you because I am fearfully and wonderfully made; your works are wonderful, I know that full well.

PSALM 139:13-14 (NIV)

Once there was a magic isle
   A place of awe and wonder
      Where sandy beaches line the shore
   And waves display their thunder

The trees were tall and leafy green
With grassy glades between
And waterfalls ran down the hills
To become clear, lazy streams

But, it's not the beauty of this place
That makes the island special
It's the animals that call it home
That burrow, graze or nestle

For, every mammal, every bird
All species 'ere created
Each reptile and amphibian
Were on this isle located

Here, life abundant knows no bounds
In all its mass and motion
Hosting feathers, fur and scales
Just like an ark upon the ocean

Of all the creatures living here
That ran or crawled or flew
None was more peculiar than
The unlikely Pandaroo

His upper half was Chinese bear
And through genetic wonder
His lower half distinctly like
A marsupial from down under

His challenges were many
To accomplish daily living
For his body parts seemed quite mismatched
Ill-suited, unforgiving

When it came to motion
He did the best that he could do
Not moving like a normal bear
He bounced like a kangaroo

But, his head and shoulders, arms and chest
Were large and much too brawny
Nothing like a kangaroo's
More thin and light and scrawny

So, when he'd lean to get a start
To make his way by hopping
The challenge wasn't getting there
The challenge now was stopping

When he reached his chosen spot
There simply were no breaks
And so, he'd stop by bouncing into
Bushes, trees and lakes

Eating was another chore
That surely was no breeze
For the leaves he loved were only found
High in the swaying trees

Can you imagine climbing high
As surely you must do
To reach these tender, budding leaves
With the feet of a kangaroo?

His greatest trial was fitting in
Belonging anywhere
He was only partial kangaroo
And not all panda bear

He'd gather with the other roos
To lie beneath the trees
But, conscious of his panda parts
He rested ill at ease

Likewise with the panda bears
He had himself to blame
He could never seem to look beyond
The ways they weren't the same

So, more and more, all by himself
In loneliness he'd sit
And think about the countless ways
He didn't seem to fit

One day, as he was feeling blue
The forest's quiet hush
Was broken by a crashing sound
Within the underbrush

Unsettled by this sudden noise
The Pandaroo just froze
And sat staring at the tree line
Where the clamoring arose

He heard somebody singing
Just as loudly as they could
The words were bright and happy
As they echoed through the woods

"I may not be a peacock
Or a lion with regal mane
But I follow the Creator
And he loves me just the same"

"Whether cloaked in neon feathers
Fur as fine as it can be
I'm always going to love
The Great Creator 'cross the sea!"

Then, bursting through the bushes
Came a creature on the scene
The most frightening . . . and funny
The Pandaroo had ever seen

His head was large and wooly
Curving horns and shaggy beard
But below its massive shoulders
Well, this animal got weird

His legs were thin and spindly
Not much thicker than a rope
He turned to face the Pandaroo
"Hello, I'm the Buffalope"

The Pandaroo was much confused
By the upper and lower half
He wasn't sure if he should run
Or stay or cry or laugh

But, the Buffalope just stood and smiled
He'd seen this all before
The startled, disbelieving looks
That everybody wore

"I hope I'm not disturbing you
I kind of lost my way"
The Buffalope, congenial
And polite began to say

"I thought I'd found a hidden trail
A short cut to the glade
But before I knew what happened
Well, it seems I must have strayed"

"No worries," said the Pandaroo
Feeling more at ease
"Why I, myself, occasionally
Bump into brush and trees"

The Buffalope gave a chuckle
In his booming baritone
"Say, I'm wondering why you're sitting
In this forest all alone?"

"Well, by now you may have noticed
I'm not quite a normal bear
I'm also not a kangaroo
I'm neither here-nor-there"

"I feel so darn self-conscious
Feel it everywhere I go
Seems the top of me is misfit
Or my legs and feet below"

"So, I find a patch of forest
That's concealed and out of sight
Here, I don't feel quite so badly
Like a failure or a blight"

The Pandaroo then dropped his head
His chin upon his chest
"I wish I wasn't different
Just the same as all the rest"

The silence fell between them
Till the Buffalope remarked
"Well, you may have noticed normal's
Not exactly where I'm parked"

"I know the hurt you're feeling
The unfairness that's conferred
I see Buffalo and antelope
And don't belong to either herd"

"But, there's something rare and special
Something only you can be
In the plan designed and driven
By the Creator 'cross the sea"

"He knows us from the inside out
Our dreams and tears and aches
He leaves nothing void and empty
And He never makes mistakes"

"It's up to us to trust Him
Find our purpose in His plan
When we do, that's when we're joyful
And really feel His loving hand"

"As for me, I've learned to follow
Seek the path He has arranged
On the outside, nothing's different
Yet, somehow, everything is changed"

The Buffalope moved closer
With some mischief in his eyes
"I'll never have to worry
Bout being called old thunder thighs"

The Pandaroo raised up his head
And laughed until he cried
The Buffalope just grinned
And pawed the ground as sadness died

And, when his laughing faded
Pandaroo quick wiped his eyes
He decided then and there
To put away his sorry "whys"

"I have to really thank you
For your words sweet and selective
You've helped improve my outlook
With a healthy new perspective"

"I never did consider
That my curse was really wealth
I guess I was too busy
Feeling sorry for myself"

"Instead of all this moping
Hiding out in isolation
I think I'll hop along
And find my place in His creation"

"Now you're talking partner!"
Buffalope saw worry fade
"Well, I'd better mosey on
And try to find that sunny glade"

"As for you, stay on the pathway
And if you find somebody blue
Just share what you've been given
So they can walk the pathway too"

With that, the shaggy bison
Legs like sticks of peppermint
Proceeded on his way
Singing loudly as he went

"Oh, I'll never be a rhino
Or a great big tall giraffe
But I can act with kindness
Find new friends and make them laugh"

"So, if you're feeling gloomy
Sing and make the sadness flee
And always seek to praise
The Great Creator 'cross the sea"

The Pandaroo then waved goodbye
Glad for the smile he wears
Then left to find the kangaroos
And seek the panda bears

The roos were napping in the shade
When Pandaroo came hopping
In his excitement he forgot
His fatal flaw, his stopping

He hooked two saplings with his arms
He twisted and he bent them
Desperate to decrease his speed
And halt his great momentum

Grabbing one with both his paws
He circled round and round
Till gravity took over
And he settled on the ground

Sheepishly he looked
To the reclining kangaroos
Not one was meanly laughing
(Although they did seem quite amused)

They asked if he was injured
With a caring, patient essence
One kangaroo spoke up
And even offered stopping lessons

The Pandaroo then saw
His former thoughts of fear and dread
Were woefully misplaced
Existing mostly in his head

He then enjoyed a quiet nap
Amongst the kangaroos
Then went in search of pandas
And their friendship to peruse

As he crossed the sunny island
Toward the high and swaying trees
He could hear the sounds of turmoil
Floating in upon the breeze

When he bounced into the meadow
Where the pandas like to sit
The bears were pacing tensely
As one mother threw a fit

He achieved a sliding halt and
Heard the mother crying, "please!"
As she pointed in her panic
High into the swaying trees

The sight where aimed her finger
Caused the Pandaroo to blanch
For there, above the meadow
A baby panda clutched a branch

"I only left him for a second
And he climbed out on that limb
It's too thin and weak to hold me
So I couldn't get to him"

"I tried and tried to coax him
But he wouldn't come to me
Oh, can't someone be a hero
Fetch my baby from the tree?"

The pandas stood in quandary
None desired her plea to snub
But all were far too heavy
For that branch that held the cub

They milled and paced and fretted
Not discerning what to do
Till one voice broke through the din
"I'll save him," cried the Pandaroo

All eyes are fixed upon him
And their gaze he bravely meets
But no panda sees his face
'Cause they're all looking at his feet

With all the looks of worry
Bravery starts to melt away
Then, he thinks about the Buffalope
And what he had to say

So, he trusts the Great Creator
Gives his all, yes, every ounce
With a cry of "cowabunga!"
Pandaroo begins to bounce

With each leap, he carries higher
Jumping up like a machine
Back to earth, then springing skyward
Like a panda trampoline

He strained his every muscle
Bouncing heedless to the breech
But, even with his best
The cub remained just out of reach

He felt his vigor failing
As his legs began to burn
He could fathom just one option
Just one place where he could turn

"Oh, Great Creator 'cross the sea"
As to the ground, he quick descended
"On the opinions of all others
For my worth I have depended"

"Please forgive that foolish notion
Make my heart and spirit new
Give me strength to do the thing
That you created me to do!"

With that prayer, he hit the meadow
And his legs coiled like a spring
Then he launched himself and aimed
Up where the baby waits and clings

In a pose like Superman
He stretched his arms for all their worth
And plucked the little panda
From his lofty tree-top perch

To the ground they both did plummet
And to keep the cub from harm
The Pandaroo safe wrapped him
In his own great panda arms

His landing was impeccable
As cheering filled his ears
He restored the cub and mother
Midst her hugs and smiles and tears

Hoisted up on panda shoulders
And then carried 'round the glade
Pandaroo felt like a hero
In this joyful bear parade

Then, he thought about the Buffalope
Where he aimed thanks and praise
The attitude and point of view
That filled his happy days

So, in the midst of celebration
He rallied up this cheering throng
And singing with one voice
He taught them all this little song

"Though the day be fraught with peril
Filled with trouble near and far
We can trust the one who loves us best
No matter who we are"

"Whether napping in the sun
Or dangling high up in a tree
Just lift your voice and praise
The Great Creator 'cross the sea"

From that day, throughout his lifetime
Pandaroo had many pals
Not just kangaroos and pandas
Also, otters, wolves and owls

But, of all the friends he'd made
Amongst the deer and gulls and squid
He loved the misfits best
The ones who felt like he once did

He remembered what the Buffalope
Had said that he should do
"Always share what you've been given
So they can walk the pathway too"

And so, this sunny day
He sought someone he'd heard about
A quiet, lonely creature
Who seemed lost in fear and doubt

Within a distant forest
Quite beyond the beaten track
There sat a little monkey
Wrapped in stripes of white and black

"Hello," he called with gusto
"I'm Pandaroo," he said with zing
Thus, he met the Chimpanzeebra
And then taught him how to sing

DEVOTIONAL THOUGHTS

I have to believe that all of us have felt left out at one time or another. That can be a really lonely feeling. Sometimes others impose that feeling on us, but I think, more-often-than-not, we impose it on ourselves. Our lack of confidence or feelings of self-consciousness create barriers or a sense of isolation where one doesn't actually exist.

If only we could see ourselves as God sees us. He didn't wait for us to be good, better or best before sending his Son to die for us. He loves us completely right where we are. And, in His hands, everything we do and everything we are can become useful and beautiful.

God doesn't make mistakes, and He has a plan laid out for each of us. Let's give Him who and what we are and leave it to Him to do good things with whatever we have to offer. No one is left out in the heart of God.

YOU DO YOUR PART, I'LL DO MINE

Sometimes God asks you to do the ridiculous

Noah was six hundred years old when the floodwaters came on the earth. And Noah and his sons and his wife and his son's wives entered the ark to escape the waters of the flood. Pairs of clean and unclean animals, of birds and of all creatures that move along the ground, male and female, came to Noah and entered the ark, as God had commanded Noah.

GENESIS 7:6-9 (NIV)

nce there was a family man
 So many years ago
 With wife and sons and spouses
 Quite like some that you may know

They farmed and planted vineyards
Nurtured crops and gardens too
And when the time for harvest came
They reaped, then sowed anew

The man was always thankful
For the gifts of earth and sod
He knew the very air he breathed
Was a precious gift from God

But, what brings him greatest pleasure
Is the fountain of his joys
The fact of being Father to
A household full of boys

A Father's love filled up his heart
And squeezed it like a boa
This honest, prosperous family man
Goes by the name of Noah

His sons all loved their Father
And he likewise cherished them
But these boys could be a handful
Names of Japheth, Ham and Shem

Japheth, who's the oldest
Always seems to be in charge
Serious and bossy
With a voice both loud and large

He's driven and he's focused
Always striving to be better
High achiever, true believer
And the consummate go-getter

Shem, the middle brother
Is a happy, funny bloke
Always ready with a story
Or a riddle or a joke

He finds something to laugh at
In most every situation
Causing family merriment
And sometimes irritation

This brings us to the youngest
Of the brothers in this clan
Unassuming, shy and quiet
Best describes the son named Ham

No paragon like Japheth
Or comedian like Shem
He never seems to measure up
A rock beside a gem

It's not for lack of trying
Or an absence of desire
Seems he's always judged just short of
What the circumstance requires

Why is Ham this way regarded?
Why's he judged so incomplete?
Well, perhaps you would be too
If you were named for sandwich meat

Ham idolizes Japheth
Seeks to work with him each day
He's trying to be helpful
But is mostly in the way

Till finally Japheth's had it
His blood pressure starts to climb
"Time to go now little brother
You do your part, I'll do mine"

Nursing damaged ego
With hurt feelings now to stem
Ham hears the sound of laughter
There he knows he'll locate Shem

And yes, Shem is surrounded
By a large, admiring crowd
As he tells them funny stories
They all roar and laugh aloud

Ham has always wished that he
Was funny like his brother
As the laughter fades from one joke
Shem begins to tell another

"Why'd the chicken cross the road?"
He asked, with grinning face
He was about to share the punch line
When his good humor was erased

Before he could proclaim it
Past the circle, someone cried
"The chicken crossed the road so
It could reach the other side!"

Shem could not believe it
As beyond the crowd he scanned
Where a smile changed fast to horror
On the face of brother, Ham

Ham had shouted out the answer
And he knew that he had blown it
He hadn't meant to steal the joke
He'd been caught up in the moment

Shem pulled young Ham aside
And gave his chest emphatic pokes
"Now listen little brother
In this clan I tell the jokes!"

"No more stealing of my thunder
No more stepping on my lines
Leave the comedy to me and
You do your part, I'll do mine"

Now the day was truly awful
What was left for him but pouting?
Ham was pondering his bad luck
When he heard his Father shouting

Ham raced back toward the house
Just like a hound called by his master
Shem and Japheth beat him there
They were, of course, much faster

As they gathered 'round their Father
He was acting very odd
His voice was filled with wonder
"I've been spoken to by God"

The boys all traded glances
Tried to cover their dismay
But old Noah never noticed
He had far too much to say

"The Lord is quite discouraged
By the evil done by men
He's going to wipe it clean
And then he's going to start again"

"The skies will fill with rain
And from the earth a flood will rise
Till the water's passed our knees, our waists
Our necks, our chins, our eyes!"

Their Father stood there panting
As his boys looked back at him
All Ham could do was worry that
He'd never learned to swim

"But, the Lord has made a way"
Said Noah, letting hope unfurl
"To spare me and my family
From his judgement on the world"

The boys just sat and listened
And their eyes with wonder filled
As he told them all about
The giant boat that they would build

Just when they had thought
This tale could not get more fantastic
Came the part about the animals
And Japheth just went spastic

"We're supposed to build an ark
And this is going to keep us dry?
We have never seen it rain
There's not a cloud up in the sky"

"If God wants us to build it
Well, he's going to have to prove it
Where will we find gopher wood?
And what the heck's a cubit?"

Shem said, "I'm with Japheth
This is nuts, this is insane
Two of every animal
To bring in from the rain?"

"Where will we find rhinos?
Cheetahs, chipmunks, hares and hogs?
Coyotes, llamas, turtles?
Chimpanzees and prairie dogs?"

Noah was discouraged
By these comments on God's plan
He was about to plead for silence
When he heard the voice of Ham

"We should listen to our Father
Trust him with our life and limb
If God would speak to any man
You know it would be him"

"The ark that Father speaks of
I think that we should build it
And the animals will come
For God himself has surely willed it"

These words made Noah smile
And also gave his brothers pause
For they were both surprised
By Ham's endorsement of this cause

They found themselves inspired
By this one they'd deemed a waif
Though lacking strength or humor
Ham exceeded them in faith

Well, soon they all got started on
Construction of their ship
Wood was sawed and hammered
And went flying off in chips

Japheth took the lead and set
A rapid pace to guide them
He was angry, as their neighbors
Gathered 'round just to deride them

But the mocking and the jeering
Was the hardest on poor Shem
For the friends he'd entertained
Were all now laughing right at him

Ham was always busy
Doing everything he could
To contribute to the building of
Their giant boat of wood

After weeks and weeks of toil
The last drops of sweat were given
The last board was now in place
The last nail had been driven

Then, Noah and his sons
With all their labor now abated
Stood back and just admired
This great ark they had created

They couldn't have more pride
Than if a million dollars bought her
Now, they just needed the animals
And they really needed water!

They waited days, then weeks, then months
But nothing seemed to change
Their neighbors now avoided them
Convinced they were deranged

Japheth's patience snapped again
He called a family meeting
His agenda carried just one thing
The plan and it's completing

"We've spent months in heavy labor
Working hard as Santa's elves
Its now clear if we're to finish
Then we must do it ourselves"

"Shem, you get the animals
Work daylight until dark
Round them up, and then we'll
Somehow get them in the ark"

"Ham, you gather food
For we must feed each hungry critter
Find lots of shovels, mops and pails
And tons of kitty litter"

"I will take the toughest job"
He went on to explain
"We really need the water
So, I'm going to make it rain!"

As if they'd felt a wizard's spell
Or drank a magic potion
Shem and Japheth left their seats
To put the plan in motion

Ham then shouted, "Stop, let's talk!"
This turn he just deplored
"We have to put our faith in God
Let's wait upon the Lord!"

But, neither brother heard his cries
They ran their separate ways
Shem, to find some animals
Japheth, storm clouds to raise

Taking drum and mallet
Putting feathers in his hair
Japheth starts to dance around
Tossed dust up in the air

He danced and drummed and threw up dirt
For over seven hours
Till finally, he fell and laid
Exhausted in the flowers

For, despite his frantic efforts
All remained arid and dry
There was no rain or drizzle
Not a cloud up in the sky

As he lay there panting
He saw Shem trudge up the road
His hair and clothes disheveled
In each hand he held a toad

"I tried to catch some squirrels
But I lost them in the trees
Then I grabbed a pair of donkeys
But they kicked me in the knees"

"I saw and chased a jackal
But I couldn't run him down
Every badger I pursued
Just simply hid under the ground"

"So, I picked up these two toads
But I feel just like a nut
Cause there's no way that I can tell if
They are boys or girls or what!"

Shem sat down next to Japheth
And they felt their failure pound them
It was here in raw frustration
Brother Ham and Noah found them

"I hope you've learned a lesson"
Said their Father to his sons
"It's the man who trusts in God who is
The man who overcomes"

"For, no impatient action
Brings fulfillment to his sentence
He wants your trust, your love, your life
Your faith and your repentance"

Then, Noah winked at Ham
And hugged his brothers both in kind
"I believe what God is saying is
You do your part, I'll do mine"

The truth that Noah spoke was clear
To both Japheth and Shem
And through their Father's love they felt
God's perfect love for them

And then, a little miracle
Took place upon that day
When his older brothers came to Ham
And both had this to say

"We owe you an apology
We know you tried to lift us
Above our vain and foolish acts
We hope you can forgive us"

"We're sorry for our selfishness
Our pride and our neglect
Know now, you have our high esteem
Our love and our respect"

These words made Ham feel ten-feet tall
And Noah filled with pride
With love, he gestured to his boys
And called them to his side

"The Lord will keep his promises
To all who will receive Him
His part involves His faithfulness
And our part - just believe Him"

As they stood together
Wiping tears out of their eyes
The ground began to shake
Beyond the hill, the dust to rise

Looking to the knoll
Up where the road is steep and bending
They scarce believe their eyes
At what they swiftly see descending

Elephants and zebra
Armadillos, kangaroo
Were walking down the hill
In perfect tandem two-by-two

Wolverines and panda bears
Camels, moose, raccoons
Porcupines, hyenas
Alligators and baboons

Amidst this great cacophony
Of roars and howls and barks
They scampered up the ramp
And disappeared into the ark

The boys stood there in disbelief
Their mouths agape in wonder
And, astonishment expanded at
The sound of distant thunder

The dust began to settle as
The sky grew still and dark
With arms around their shoulders
Noah led them to the ark

They climbed the ramp, and Noah paused
To scan the arid plain
And as he turned to go inside
He felt a drop of rain…

DEVOTIONAL THOUGHTS

Can you imagine what it would have been like to be one of Noah's sons? There you are, living your life and minding your own business in the middle of the desert when Dad comes home with some news. God has spoken to him. Okay… God says there's going to be a flood, even though it has never rained before. Okay… God says we're to build a huge ship in the middle of the desert so we can escape the flood. Okay… Oh yes, and God says that two of every animal on earth is coming with us.

How much faith and how much patience did it take for them to obey the commands of God? This, in the face of certain ridicule from their neighbors. Although we may never be asked to build an ark in the middle of the desert, God still speaks to His people and does miracles on the foundation of their faith. Our part is to listen for the voice of God and obey. God's part is to supply the miracle.

If we do our part, God promises to do His. Are you being called to do something that seems impossible? Day by day, keep your eyes on Him. Look for the small acts of faithfulness that are ours each day. Let these encourage you to know that God will always finish what he starts.

STEVE THE SHEEP

Why do we wander from the shepherd who loves us?

Suppose one of you has a hundred sheep and loses one of them.
Does he not leave the ninety-nine in the open country
and go after the lost sheep until he finds it?

LUKE 15:4 (NIV)

It's a warm and lazy summer day
With wispy clouds unspooling
The sun shines brightly overhead
The wind is light and cooling

It's on this breeze, a sound is heard
So faint you just can hear it
It makes one want to take a walk
To try and get more near it

So, we stroll beyond the trees
Across a little brook
Then up a hill, and down again
To have ourselves a look

There, scattered on the hillside
Where the slope is not too steep
The sound that birthed our little quest
Comes from a flock of sheep

Their "baas" seem so contented
As they move across the glade
Feasting on the lush, green grass
Each yummy, scrumptious blade

We scan the flock from left-to-right
And when the counting's done
The total rams and lambs and ewes
Is ninety-nine...plus one

I say "plus one," for if you look
Across the sunny vale
You'll see one sheep is wandering there
And herein lies our tale

We head in that direction now
As through the flock we weave
With hurried pace, we're face-to-face
And meet the sheep named Steve

This sunny day's made just for him
Or so it surely seems
To romp and play, or simply lay
Lost in his sheep day dreams

Yes, Steve's is feeling quite relaxed
He fears no bear or leopard
He knows that watching 'ore the flock
Is the ever-faithful shepherd

The shepherd leads them to the ground
Where sweetest waters flow
Whether high-up on the hillside
Or the pastures down below

He establishes their boundaries
Where they can run or eat or lie
And so, they pass contented days
Beneath his watchful eye

What a peaceful, safe existence
From the morning to the eve
So, why relate this little tale?
That brings us back to Steve

It's not that he's rebellious
No, that's not the tag that fits him
He just gets a little careless
When the mood to wander hits him

He also can't conceive of
What the fuss is all about
When the shepherd sets his limits
He's been known to whine and pout

"I'm not a little spring lamb
I know just as well as He
Where to eat and where to drink
What's good or bad for me"

"It's not like I will run away
The rules, I mostly heed 'em
I'm not hurting anybody
I just want a little freedom"

For, the shepherd, just that morning
Had laid out their bound-a-ries
They were not to go beyond the brook
Nor past the line of trees

"The brook is swift and running cold"
The caring shepherd warned
"While in the woods live creatures
That may seek to do you harm"

"So, stay here in the sunshine
And the day will be just fine"
The sheep "baaed" their agreement
Well, at least the ninety-nine

For Steve had spied some flowers
Caught their scent upon the breeze
And he'd quickly wandered over
Where the meadow meets the trees

He sniffed the violet petals
Then the yellow down below
Was about to smell the red ones
When the woods rang with "Hello"

Steve raised his head in wonder
He could see no face or form
As a voice came from the shadows
"My, the day has turned quite warm"

"It has," said Steve now blinking
From the sunshine in the glade
Said the voice, "It's so much cooler
There's no sun here in the shade"

"Why don't you come and rest awhile
And get out of this heat
There's better grass beyond these trees
And a stream to cool your feet"

Steve said, somewhat sheepishly
"I cannot leave the grass
No, the shepherd wouldn't like it
If beyond the trees I passed"

The voice said, "Yes, the shepherd…"
And the tone held some derision
"Must you always follow orders?
Can't you make your own decisions?"

"As for me, I'm heading over
To that pasture cool and fair
If you ever feel grown up enough
Perhaps I'll see you there"

Steve's pose was one of puzzlement
There standing on the lawn
His "Hellos" all went unanswered
It was clear the voice was gone

So, Steve began to ponder
For the voice had made him think
As his will grew up within him
His good sense began to shrink

"I could scout a new horizon
Find fresh grass for us to eat
I'd just walk until I found it
And then beat a quick retreat"

"Why, I could be a hero
And the shepherd, he will see
That I can make decisions
He can put his trust in me"

Steve then squared his shoulders
And he slowly bent his knees
Taking one last look behind him
He then walked into the trees

There was a kind of trail here
And it turned this way and that
Leading further from the pasture
Where the sheep and shepherd sat

Rocks obscured the pathway
Making Steve step up-and-over
The ground was hard and full of weeds
There was no grass or clover

Second thoughts and worries
Clouded Steve's determination
This sheep that strode with bravado
Now paused with hesitation

The sun was soon diminished
By the canopy of leaves
Can you hear that thumping heartbeat?
Have no doubt, that heart is Steve's

As his fears assailed him
He considered turning 'round
But he felt himself now sink
In what he'd thought was solid ground

He'd walked into a bog! Oh no!
T'was filled with mud and slime
He struggled hard to reach the edge
He tried and tried to climb

He thought that he might perish
Then he lunged with all his might
With this heave, he left the bog
But, oh now, wasn't he a sight!

His wool was dank and matted
Why, it made him look obese
For the muddy, filthy water
Had been soaked-up by his fleece

So great now was his misery
The worst he'd ever known
He choked upon a sob and said
"That's it, I'm going home!"

He started his departure
And then found to his dismay
That he hadn't paid attention
And he didn't know the way

As he stood in desperation
What came rushing to his head
Were the warnings and instructions
All the words the shepherd said

"If only he would find me
Everything would be ok
I'd never wander off again
I'd never disobey"

"I'll listen and I'll honor
All the things you ask me to
Oh please, please come and find me
And I'll follow only you"

He promised and he promised
And when his pledge was done
He heard a voice behind him say
"Hello my little one"

He turned in joy and laughter
Then felt the blood within him freeze
For t'was not the shepherd speaking
T'was the voice from in the trees

Steve finally could see him
And the sight filled him with dread
That pointed nose, the bushy tail
And coat of brightest red

He'd heard the shepherd speak about
The one who sneaks and stalks
And here he was now facing
His worst nightmare - called the fox

"My my, it's just so easy"
Said the fox, his manner cool
"To convince someone they're brilliant
When in truth, they're just a fool"

"To leave the sun and safety"
He now mocked with his demeanor
"Don't you know the oldest gimmick
Is to promise grass that's greener?"

"I'll tell you now my secret"
And he winked in mocking jest
"I just plant some discontentment
It's your pride that does the rest"

Poor Steve could only stand there
And he cried, because he knew
That despite the cruel taunting
All the fox had said was true

"I'll stop now," said the fox
"For I detect I've pushed your buttons
As much as I like talking
I so much more enjoy mutton!"

As the fox began advancing
And poor Steve was locked in dread
Something whistled through the air
And barely missed the fox's head

The shepherd stepped beside him!
Before Steve could say a thing
He had reached into his bag
And slipped a stone into his sling

He swung the weapon deftly
But before the arc was done
The fox gave out a cry
And ran as fast as he could run

Steve could scarce believe it
As he shouted his elation
Looking over to the shepherd
With great thanks and admiration

Then, he suddenly remembered
All the trouble he had caused
His smile turned quickly downward
And his celebration paused

He eyes now filled with falling tears
He slowly dropped his head
Feeling sorry and ashamed for
All the things he'd thought and said

The shepherd softly smiled
And with his eyes consumed with grace
He knelt and touched Steve's trembling chin
And lifted up his face

"There you are my precious one
My wandering little waif
The fox is gone, and I'm right here
Don't cry now, you are safe"

"I'm not crying 'cause I'm frightened"
Poor Steve blubbered, and he brayed
"I'm crying, 'cause I let you down
I failed, I disobeyed"

"You set your expectations
And you gave us our instructions
But I chose my own ambitions
My opinions, my deductions"

Then, Steve dissolved in silence
And the shepherd gently said
"Let's don't talk about your failures
But the truth you've learned instead"

"I don't set my expectations
To put mindless rules above you
I do, because you're precious
I do, because I love you"

Steve looked up believing
He was as loved as he could be
For grace had boldly saved him
And the truth had set him free

The shepherd hugged him tightly
There among the trees and boulders
And with his mighty, loving arms
Lifted Steve upon his shoulders

"Now you know me," said the shepherd
"And you know that you are mine
So, hang on tight my small one
Let's rejoin the ninety-nine"

Well, time has come and gone
Since Steve's adventure in the woods
All the shepherd's words he heeds
Because he knows they're for his good

For, Steve has learned the lesson
Understood by all the bright ones
Freedom's not the lack of boundaries
It's submitting to the right ones

DEVOTIONAL THOUGHTS

The shepherd and his sheep is one of the most endearing images Jesus employed to describe our relationship with Him, the Good Shepherd. Green pastures, still waters, and a rod and staff to comfort and defend us. These create feelings of peace, provision and protection. So, here's the $64,000 question: Why do we wander away from a Savior who loves us? Steve's story gives us a few clues. Pride, a false sense of independence, chaffing under restrictions or boundaries; or simply not paying attention.

As Steve discovered, the boundaries and expectations established by the shepherd were there to keep him safe and well. And so, it is with us. Just as a loving parent will place boundaries around their children, so our Heavenly Father places boundaries around us. It greatly benefits us to learn and submit to those expectations. Just ask Steve, it's a lesson learned by all the bright ones!

FLAWLESS

How does God see us?

For all have sinned and fall short of the glory of God, and are justified freely by his grace through the redemption that came by Jesus Christ.

ROMANS 3:23-24 (NIV)

The cobblestones are gleaming wet
From an early morning rain
Overhead's the rhythmic clatter
Of the elevated train

The sidewalk's lined with sandwich boards
Each striving to declare
That here you'll find a grocer
Tailor, watch or shoe repair

And, just beyond the butcher shop
You see the yellow door?
It marks the small emporium
That's Rothman's Jewelry Store

Dawn peeks through the windows
And around each half-drawn shade
Casting dusty beams of sunlight on
The silver, gold and jade

Old buffed and polished oaken floors
Host displays of wood and brass
Both inviting and protective
Where small locks guard doors of glass

On beds of soft, black velvet
And enthroned like kings and queens
Lie necklaces and pendants
Broaches, bracelets, pins and rings

Here countless gems have traded hands
For sweethearts, wives and mothers
Purchased by a countless stream of
Husbands, beaus and brothers

And, all transactions large and small
All lay-a-ways and buys
Each sale of jewelry has transpired
Under old-man Rothman's eyes

Those eyes are slowly dimming now
The same with what he hears
Yet, every day he's where he's been
For forty-seven years

In suit and vest, a tie to match
His footsteps rise and drop
As he descends the stairway
From his room above the shop

The window shades rise one-by-one
A new day is exposed
He unlocks the door, and flips the sign
Reading "open" now, not "closed"

He tucks a rose in his lapel
At exactly nine-oh-three
And awaits the day's first customers
While he enjoys a cup of tea

The displays around the jewelry store
Are positively jammed
With gems acquired in Singapore
Hong Kong and Amsterdam

Upon each case, a lettered sign
White with crimson trim
Informs the reader as to what
Appears for sale within

Here, emeralds and diamonds
And amethysts are sold
While across the floor, is topaz
Rubies, platinum and gold

Yet, there's one case unlike the rest
In back, and to the right
When the Jeweler shines this furniture
He works with awed delight

The wood is deep mahogany
And carved and tooled by hand
The hinges, lock and metal clasp
Forged expertly and grand

The velvet holds no dust or lint
Superbly squared and leveled
The translucent beauty of the glass
Is etched and deeply beveled

What makes this case unique within
This shop so dignified?
It's the emptiness that's so distinct
No jewelry rests inside

No sapphires, garnets, emeralds
No onyx or tourmaline
No diamonds, rubies, opals, turquoise
Topaz or aquamarine

The reason for the absent gems
Is simple to define
The vacancy? A single word
Found on this case's sign

This word defines criteria
For gems herein displayed
That single word is "Flawless"
And no stone has made this grade

This case, sitting empty for decades
And cold as an unused church
Was placed here by old-man Rothman
The result of his life-long search

For, over his many decades
Countless gems he has scrutinized
Yet, not one has met this standard
Under his firm and discerning eye

As to flaws, he knows their signature
How they masquerade in the gleam
Some subtle, and just barely showing
Others clear, and quite plainly seen

Imperfections that cannot be altered
Erased, removed or abated
They're birthed within the very core
From the time the stone is created

He's known gems with flaws by the hundreds
And others with barely a trace
But, whether one or one-hundred-thousand
None can enter the flawless case

Yet, the jeweler, gemstone by gemstone
Continues his dogged pursuit
Insistently seeking perfection
In a quest that has borne him no fruit

But, today his thoughts lie elsewhere
Bringing pleasure to him as they run
He's joyfully anticipating
The return of his only Son

He's completed a journey of study
To continents both far and wide
His Father's been tracking his odyssey
On a map that he keeps at his side

It's filled with arrows and circles
With notes, and with commenting lines
From one end-of-the-earth to the other
Capturing passion, commitment and time

He has traveled the world seeking knowledge
Studying gems both precious and rare
His authority now is unchallenged
His reputation beyond all compare

And his Father, as proud as a peacock
Sometimes can scarcely believe
He's about to grasp a precious dream
He has sought his whole life to achieve

For, the Son will step in with the Father
Long ago they established this plan
When he left he was just beyond boyhood
He now returns an accomplished young man

Then, suddenly pulled from his reverie
By the sound of the bell 'ore the door
His Son steps in from the sidewalk
And quickly he crosses the floor

Now a hug, and emotional welcome
Then his Son hangs his jacket and hat
As Rothman refreshes the teapot
They lean on the counter and chat

For hours they talk of his travels
His studies, his many degrees
Occasionally serving a customer
Then resuming their talk over tea

So, the shadows grow long as the evening
Descends on the shop like a blind
Then, the Son casts his eyes to the corner
And the case with the old "Flawless" sign

"I see it still sits cold and empty"
As he moves close beside the display
Its beauty, just as he'd remembered
Its futility firmly conveyed

He picks up the sign on the cover
And smiling, he fingers the word
This unyielding, exacting requirement
The isolation its meaning's assured

"When I opened this shop, I was your age"
Said his Father, behind tired eyes
"That sign represented my values
My commitment to not compromise"

"My desire was to deal in perfection
Without blemish, or error, or flaw
What I found was decidedly different"
As his voice became quiet and raw

"My work is concluding in failure
As that case everyday lets me know
In these stones, there's no sign of perfection
And I fear it will always be so"

As his words trailed off into silence
His Son put the sign back in place
Then, stepped over to talk with his Father
And he spoke with a smile on his face

"It's true that to look for perfection
Is a quest that is futile and drab
The only gems that will ever be flawless
Are fake, and produced in a lab"

"If I've learned anything in my studies
The education you bade me to seek
It's every stone carries some imperfection
That's what makes them each rare and unique"

"The key is to look for the beauty
And forgive when a blemish is showing
Judge the gems with a grace-filled perspective
And that case will be soon overflowing"

They locked eyes, and then nodded together
And both knew a new thing had begun
The standard upheld by the Father
Realized through the work of the Son

Then, Rothman and Son walked together
To that case in the back of the store
With a laugh, they removed the old signage
Took a key and unlocked the glass door

DEVOTIONAL THOUGHTS

Grace is an amazing thing. Often, I think, it's one of those "church words" that is said without a deep understanding of its meaning. God's perfection and our imperfection can't reside together. By its very nature, perfection is eliminated when imperfection is introduced. Think of it this way. Say you had a swimming pool full of perfectly pure water, no pollutants, no chemicals. If you poured fifty-gallons of sludge into this water, obviously it would no longer be pure. But, what if you added a single drop of sludge to this water? Would it still be pure? The answer is no. Any trace of pollution means the entire body of water is impure. Purity and impurity simply can't reside in the same space.

Our sin, our flesh, renders us impure. This is what creates the separation between mankind and a perfect God. And, as with the example of the water, it doesn't matter if it's one sin or one-million sins. The perfect and the imperfect are separated. God loved us too much to leave things this way.

It's the sacrifice of Jesus Christ, on our behalf, that gives God the ability to see us not through our sin, but through the forgiving, purifying and reconciling blood of His Son, shed for this very purpose. Grace is God's purifier. And, grace is a gift. I invite you to accept and receive the grace God offers through His Son, Jesus. When we do, God, our Father, sees us as flawless.

AN AMERICAN PARABLE

A story of grace

About the eleventh hour he went out and found still others standing around. He asked them "Why have you been standing here all day long doing nothing?" "Because no one has hired us" they answered.

MATTHEW 20:6-7 (NIV)

ave you ever lain within your bed
Awake, but with closed eyes?
You know the sky is lightening
And the time has come to rise

Yet, there you lay beneath the sheet
You hear the tick and tock
What would you give if you'd the chance
To freeze that blasted clock

Left up to you, you'd slip back to
That dream about the beach
But as with dreams, it softly fades
And stays just out of reach

You name and then eliminate
Each excuse to stay in bed
When these reasons are exhausted
Only then, you lift your head

The morning air is chilly
So's the floor beneath your feet
You shuffle to the kitchen
Just to make something to eat

There, sitting at the table
With a half-sipped glass of water
Is why you finally rose from bed
Your smiling, lovely daughter

She brightly chirps, "Hi Daddy"
It's a greeting straight from heaven
You can't believe she's grown so big
Next week she will be seven

You kiss her on the forehead
Her scent, a flower petal
Despite the cold, she warms the room
As you move to fill the kettle

You search for bread for toasting
What's left? One slice, one heel
Your back's kept to the table
So your worried look's concealed

For, you'll never let her see it
Never let her share your trial
By the time you reach the table
Digging deep, you find a smile

You set a plate before her
And exchanging tickling touches
You move to share her breakfast
Careful not to bump her crutches

They lean against the table
As you slide around behind her
She doesn't really notice
As you dodge those grim reminders

It's near two years they've been with her
She never does complain
Or comment on the accident
That's caused you so much pain

You think about her Mother
And the note she left behind
That feeling that your world was
Spinning only to unwind

You shake your head, and sip your tea
No profit in these thoughts
The rent is due, there's bills to pay
Don't tie yourself in knots

You're rescued from your thinking
By the one that you love most
For, she's telling you a little tale
Between her bites of toast

"Daddy, Grandma read me a story
From a very special book
I really, really liked it"
As she spoke, her finger shook

"You should read it to me
Grandma said you have one too
It's about a man from long ago
Who everybody knew"

"He really loved the children
When all others would forget them
Some tried to chase the kids away
But the nice man wouldn't let them"

"Grandma told me all about it
It was just before my nap
He sat upon a rock and
Let the kids sit on his lap"

"He'd pick them up and hold them
At the place called Galilee
And Grandma said if I'd been there
He would have carried me"

"It made me glad to think of it
I have been ever since
Will you read it to me?"
Her request held such suspense

"I don't know if I can find it"
You tell your little lie
For, you know it's in your closet
On the shelf above your ties

You remember when you put it there
That was such an awful night
When in anger and frustration
You just shoved it out of sight

"Well, I will look while you're at work"
Her joy was plain to see
"When you get home, we'll snuggle-up
And you can read to me"

You're thankful when the doorbell rings
And you can move to answer
While in her chair, she sings a song
And dreams that she's a dancer

Through the door comes Grandma
As she does most every day
You grab your hat, put on your coat
Prepared to make your way

You gently hug your Mother
And kiss your little girl
They both call out "good luck" to you
As you step-out in the world

Down four-flights, you quickly move
You take the stairs by twos
Stepping over refuse and
Discarded fifths of booze

Then, out the door and down the street
Around and up the hill
Your breath creates soft puffs of white
In the morning's icy chill

Down the hill, around the bend
You see your target corner
Already men are gathered
Like a churchyard full of mourners

Their hands are shoved in pockets
And their collars turned up high
Each man a stark reminder
Of how hard you'll have to try

As you join the milling throng
Just outside a wooden shed
A booming voice is rising
From the man they call Big Ed

"Alright you men, now gather 'round
The trucks will soon be here
You know the drill, no man gets work
Except through me, that clear?"

"So, form a line and pony up
You better make it good"
As he spoke, the trucks arrived
With each half-filled with wood

So, one-by-one the huddled mass
Starts moving towards the trucks
Before they climb aboard, each man
Gives Ed some hard-earned bucks

As you advance, your eyes just burn
And tear up in their sockets
Because you know you're carrying
No money in your pockets

And, with each man who pays and goes
Your heart is filled with dread
For soon, you stand with empty hands
And have to face Big Ed

Right now, you have no money
But the boss should pay today
You promise Ed you'll double
What you normally would pay

"What am I, a charity?"
Ed gives his thumb a jerk
"If you ain't got no money
Then my friend, you got no work"

He pushes you aside
And then hollers out, "That's all!"
The gates close on the trucks
And then away they slowly crawl

You stand there on the corner
With the others who are broke
One-by-one, they walk away
No voices, no one spoke

You hurry to the brickyard
For there may be something there
But, the foreman says he's sorry
Open jobs are really rare

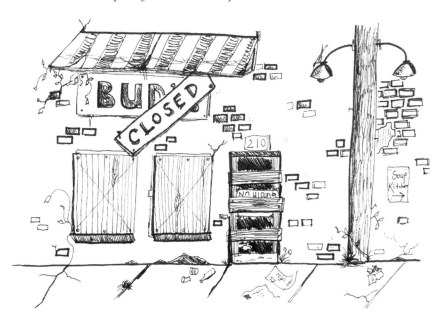

It's the same down at the bakery
And at the lumber mill
There's no work found at the stockyards
Or at the bar-and-grill

The morning turns to afternoon
Your shoes feel worn right through
You can't conceive of going
Without bread or soup or stew

Despair begins to raise its head
You know the signs of warning
You walk back to the corner where
You first began your morning

As you stand there, out of options
And not knowing what to do
A truck pulls up, a man leans out
And hollers out, "Hey you"

You nod and hurry over
Just as quickly as you can
And he inquires, "You want some work?
We need another man"

"The pay won't be too hefty"
As his voice got low and dour
"If you're interested and willing
We can work you for an hour"

With a "Yes," and with a handshake
You leap into the back
The truck moves down the roadway
As you sit on burlap sacks

When you reach the destination
You can see, off to your right
Big Ed and all the fellas
Are at work on this jobsite

The Foreman calls you over
And he shows you what to do
You're fresh, and so the task's complete
Just as your hour is through

A whistle's blowing loudly
All the men put down their tools
Their foreheads bead with sweat
Just like a thousand little jewels

The Foreman sets a table up
On which the roster's laid
The men fall in to form a line
Excited to be paid

"Attention," calls the Foreman
And the men respect his power
"I'll start with wages for the man
Who worked the last shift hour"

You walk up to the table
Past Big Ed and all the boys
The Foreman has an envelope
His face seems full of joy

He moves to hand it over
He's the boss, and so respected
It feels far too substantial
And much more than you expected

You tell the smiling Foreman
That there must be some mistake
For, you only worked an hour
There's more here than you should make

"I really like your attitude
And how you work your way
To acknowledge your good effort here
Your wage is for the day"

He reaches out to shake your hand
This means so much to you
"I'll expect you back tomorrow
We've got so much work to do"

You move beyond the table
Feeling lighter than a feather
While, behind you, Big Ed laughs out-loud
And rubs his hands together

"Imagine boys," Big Ed exclaims
"If he fulfills his hopes
Is there any doubt that we'll be pleased
With our pay envelopes"

Then, one-by-one the men were paid
But their laughter came to sputter
For, the wage they got was for the day
They began to whine and mutter

Big Ed walks to the foreman
With a visage dark and grim
"Excuse me, but it isn't fair
We're paid the same as him?"

"I've been here since the morning
Now the sun is going down
This is not what I expect
Much more here should be found"

"Why are you dissatisfied?
You're paid as we'd agreed"
He sensed a darkness in this man
The avarice and greed

"I kept right to our bargain
And my word was straight and true
If I am generous with him
What's that to do with you?"

Big Ed, he had no argument
No leg on which to stand
He turned and strode out angrily
His pay clinched in his hand

As you climb into the truck
The other men do too
Big Ed's the last to jump in back
You feel his eyes on you

And, when you reach the corner
It is very nearly dark
The trucks pull up with squealing brakes
The men all disembark

You turn to start your journey home
As dusk grows ever colder
But, before you move a single step
A hand lays on your shoulder

"I think we've got some business"
Says Big Ed, his presence trouble
"I accept the early offer
That you made to pay me double"

"I'm sure you've just forgotten
So I thought that I'd remind you"
As his words hung in the air
You sensed some men move in behind you

As you quickly lose your options
Between the choice of fight or flee
Big Ed leans close, and smiling says
"Ok, what will it be?"

Surrounded by a dozen men
And confronted by this baddie
The tension's sharply broken
As a voice calls out, "Hi Daddy"

The head of every man is turned
Surprise is so complete
As a little girl on crutches
Makes her way across the street

"Grandma said that we could come
That you would think it's nice
I hope that you are proud of me
I only rested twice"

"I might need help as we walk home"
The men all heard her say
"Maybe you could carry me
A little of the way?"

It was then, your daughter noticed
All the men around her Dad
She thought just for a second
Then she brightly spoke to add

"These men must be your friends
Why, I'm so happy I can greet you
It's really good to know you all
I'm very glad to meet you"

"Next week I have a birthday!"
She exclaimed, now so excited
"I know my Dad won't mind
If I proclaim you're all invited"

The men had dropped their eyes
And all were shuffling their feet
That is except for Ed
Who found this charming child a treat

"Oh, now my little darlin'"
And his laugh was rich and hearty
"You don't want this bunch of roughnecks
To attend your birthday party"

"You are sweet and generous
And I feel you have unmasked me
For you have given me a gift
Because you kindly asked me"

"So, thank you little missy
You have made this gang so glad
I hope we get to meet again
You go home now with your Dad"

Big Ed then looks right at you
Cracks a smile and gives a wink
"Come on you scurvy lads," he calls
"Let's get ourselves a drink"

Big Ed and all his followers
Go laughing down the street
You kneel and hug your daughter
Nothing feels quite so complete

For, life still has its lessons
Yes, no matter breadth or length
For in our greatest weakness
God will show his greatest strength

You put her on your shoulders
With her Grandma by your side
And start the journey home
With a new bounce found in your stride

"Daddy, I just remembered
I really, really looked
Although I searched for hours
I couldn't find that special book"

You smile and look up skyward
For there's no greater love than His
"Don't worry little sweetheart
I know exactly where it is"

DEVOTIONAL THOUGHTS

As a young person, I can recall reading Jesus's Parable of the Vineyard Workers (Matthew 20:1-16) and feeling a bit upset. "Why in the heck did the guys working only one hour get paid the same as those who worked all day?" That question was likely followed by my perineal favorite observation "That's not fair!"

I think it was only with some age, experience and maturity that what Jesus was trying to teach came clear. No one was "ripped off" here. The all-day workers got exactly what was promised to them – a day's wage. Unfortunately, these workers compared their paychecks with workers with whom the vineyard owner chose to be generous. Suddenly, a situation that was fine moments ago was no longer fine.

Once we begin judging the quality of our circumstances based on a comparison with others, we are on a slippery slope to jealousy and discontentment. When we view our circumstances through our relationship with Christ, we know that He will meet all our needs according to His love, mercy and grace. When we find our fulfillment and contentment in Him, we don't need to look for it elsewhere. What freedom.

The second lesson from this parable is, we don't always know the detail of another's situation. Someone who appears to be gaining something extra probably has a back story we know nothing about. Let's allow God to be the great "leveler," which frees us to rejoice for those who may get a good break. That's the recipe for thankfulness and contentment.

A DOG NAMED TONGUE

Uh oh, Gossip the cat lives right next door…

All kinds of animals, birds, reptiles and creatures of the sea are being tamed and have been tamed by man, but no man can tame the tongue. It is a restless evil, full of deadly poison.

JAMES 3:7-8 (NIV)

A horse is deftly mastered
By a single, simple bit
A rudder, modest in its size
Can steer a mighty ship

A tiny spark, carelessly flown
May devastate a forest
One voice that sings a song off key
Can spoil a merry chorus

Examples of a principle
A thing that none can tame
And spelled out very clearly
In the Bible (book of James)

For now, a story beckons
Yes, a tale has just begun
About a boy named Ronald
And his hound-dog name of Tongue

It seemed that Ron had been with Tongue
Since he could fair remember
When he got him as a Christmas gift
Some long ago December

His name was plainly obvious
More so than names before
For, his tongue was pink and lolling
And hung half-way to the floor

When Tongue was just a pup
Ron quickly had him fetching sticks
Rolling over, playing dead
And lots of other fancy tricks

He could shake, and he could speak
He could beg, and he could lay
He could hunt, and he could seek
Or he could sit, and he could stay

Yet, no matter how committed
To his discipline he clung
Ron soon was to discover
He couldn't fully tame his Tongue

For his dog, born with a nature
That unstructured time exposes
Spent one sunny afternoon
Digging-up Ron's Mother's roses

And, as Ron took up a shovel
To replace his Mother's plants
Tongue wandered to the house
And chewed his Father's favorite pants!

As his Father's angry cries
Throughout the household loudly rung
Ron tried to strategize
How he could reason with his Tongue

So, escorting now his dog
Out to the shed for a discussion
Ron patiently explained
Each bad behavioral repercussion

He laid it out in spades
So Tongue would get it in his head
And the dog seemed to agree
With every word that Ronald said

Tongue received obediently
His master's admonition
Making sorry sad-dog eyes
And softly whining his contrition

Till Ron was satisfied
That Tongue had finally got the message
And had purged the deviltry
From his behavior, every vestige

Well, for many peaceful days
No masticated pants or shoes
All the roses stayed in place
Nothing gnawed, uprooted, chewed

So, Ron's diligence relaxed
His dog was different now, assuredly
But, in truth, he'd just been lulled
Into a false sense of security

He learned this fact the hard way
About letting down your guard
When there rose a great hubbub
Next door in Mrs. Murphy's yard

It was much too nice a day
For canine chaos to commence
But it seems Tongue's dug a hole
And made his way beneath the fence

And, the point of his adventure?
Why the peace was trampled flat?
It was Tongue's pursuit of Gossip
(Who was Mrs. Murphy's cat)

Gossip walked the fence-top
Where he teased and where he taunted
Till soon it reached a point where
Gossip's all Tongue really wanted

Obsessed now with his quarry
And forgetting all his training
The dog began to dig
With every haunch and muscle straining

And Gossip, from his perch
Saw that he'd overplayed his hand
As Tongue dug like a gopher
Moving quantities of sand

Soon, Tongue's broad head emerged
And Gossip beat a fast retreat
Just as quick, the dog was under
Barking, scrambling to his feet

The chase was wild and epic
Circling thrice around the lawn
Then it moved into the flowers
Every petal quickly gone

Then, up onto the patio
These two combatants flew
Sending chairs and tables flying
Knocking down the bar-b-que

Gossip ran and ran
That cat could make a sprinter jealous
With a leap, he wound up landing
Halfway up the garden trellis

His pursuer never flinched
And with his speed both gift and gratis
Tongue also made that leap
And busted right on through the lattice

Their race detached the drainpipe
Spilled the trash-cans, split the screen
It was the craziest pursuit
This neighborhood had ever seen

Until finally, Gossip slowed
He'd run as far as he was able
And Tongue now had him trapped against
The upset picnic table

His triumph was at hand
If Tongue were able, he would holler
He was just about to pounce
When someone grabbed him by the collar

For, Ron had jumped the fence
Had seen this mad adventure's toll
As Mrs. Murphy shouted
"Get your Tongue under control!"

Apologizing now
Ron lifts his dog, secures his paws
And promises to help with
All the damage he has caused

In the days and weeks that pass
Ron really feels he's found his niche
He's employing love-filled boundaries
(And one very sturdy leash)

He works and trains his dog
But not believing for one minute
He can ever fully quell
The basic nature that's within it

So, in one corner of his yard
Our Ron has built a sturdy pen
It's his job to see that Tongue
Will never run amok again

For now, he knows the carnage
All the things that can be wrecked
When carelessly you go your way
And leave your Tongue unchecked

And what of Mrs. Murphy's cat?
Has that feline learned a lesson?
Seen the error of his ways
No more divisive moves or messin'

If that cat has changed or not
Well, I don't know, it seems toss up
And the moral of our story?
Don't let your Tongue chase after Gossip

DEVOTIONAL THOUGHTS

Is there any organ in the body quite like the tongue? The book of James 3:9 observes that *"with it we praise our Lord and Father, and with it we curse men who have been made in God's likeness."* The tongue seems to be emblematic of all the good and the bad that we, as humans, are capable of.

As Christians, we may find ourselves somewhat in control over the "big" sins of the tongue re: swearing, lying, dirty jokes or stories, insults, etc. But, often it's the subtler sins of the tongue that can trip us up: half-truths, gossip, bragging, put-downs, etc.

For as long as we walk this earth, we will need to be on guard against the sins and failings of this small yet mighty part of our bodies. Each day, we need to invite the Lord to be the master of our tongues. Especially in those areas that may seem subtle and small, but can wreak havoc on our testimony - and on those around us. Let's strive to have our tongues be instruments of encouragement, peace and blessing. God has chosen us to be his messengers. Let's speak in a manner worthy of that calling.

GABRIELLA'S SHOES

The power of a Father's love

As a father has compassion on his children, so the Lord has compassion on those who fear him; for he knows how we are formed, he remembers that we are dust. As for a man, his days are like grass, he flourishes like a flower of the field; the wind blows over it and it is gone, and its place remembers it no more.

PSALM 103:13-16 (NIV)

A little girl's bedroom
Is a rare and magic place
When the world is big and scary
Here it's warm, and snug, and safe

No ugly, frightening monsters
Ever penetrate these walls
Just teddy bears and puppets
Stuffed animals and dolls

Some days, this is a castle
Or, a house up in the trees
It's where all the bedroom tenants
Are served sandwiches and teas

It's a large and spacious ballroom
For a formal dance or prom
Or a cozy little kitchen
Perfect for a pint-sized mom

When imagination's resting
And this room is just a room
It holds the pieces of her life
Safe as a baby in the womb

For all her special things
Seems each one has a special place
On a shelf, or in a shoebox
Tied with ribbon, wrapped in lace

A ballerina music box
Atop a chest of drawers
On the window sill, are seashells
That she picked up on the shore

On the wall, you'll find her artwork
(She likes to draw when she is sad)
Next to a pin-board full of photos
From her last visit with her Dad

But, of all the rare possessions
That are special to this girl
There is something here most treasured
More than any in the world

For, deep within her closet
'Neath a quilt of reds and blues
Behind her skates and backpack
Are Gabriella's shoes

They were a present for her birthday
Wrapped in pink, a bow to match
They lie in the box they came in
Bits of pink paper still attached

Her Father bought them for her
He hadn't wrapped them, how'd she know?
Well, he could never cut the paper right
And was hopeless with a bow

She'd seen her Mother do the wrapping
Seen her look of keen vexation
For she knew quite well her husband
Would not attend the celebration

Her Mother made her worry
She seemed sad right to her core
Her face held lines and creases
Never carried there before

Though she tried with all her might
T'was too much for her to fix
There's only so much you can do
When you're just a girl of six

So, each night she'd say her prayers
Close her eyes, and just believe
And think about the days
Before her Father had to leave

There were picnics at the ocean
What happy times they'd had
When she arranged her gathered seashells
And spelled "I love you" for her Dad

They'd wrestle on the carpet
Where he'd tickle and he'd hug her
Or, they'd go to baseball games
(Those days he'd always call her "slugger")

And, gathered on his lap
In his chair, so soft and deep
He'd tell her tales of kings and princes
Till she'd finally fall asleep

Those were magic, happy times
All any girl could ever wish
Then came the day the telephone rang
And her Mother cried, and dropped a dish

Later that same evening
Her parents, hand in hand
Had a tearful conversation
She could scarcely understand

And when, after a story
Her Father carried her to bed
He seemed to hold her extra tightly
Against his neck, she laid her head

When they came into her room
He gently set her on the floor
Then he smiled, and did the thing he'd done
A hundred times before

He reached over to the dresser
Opened up the music box
And she giggled as they danced there
With her feet atop his sox

As the days passed into weeks
He spent more hours in his chair
When she hugged him, he felt thin
He began to lose his hair

Story time was very different
With the tales now told by Mom
Her Dad, under a blanket
In an effort to keep warm

Until one day, a sitter came
(Their teenage neighbor, Joan)
Her parents left, were gone for hours
Then Mom came home alone

"Daddy's sleeping over"
And the two sat down together
"While the doctors try to help him
And to make him feel all better"

"We can go and visit
Tomorrow, or the day after
He really needs his little girl
To bring her smile and laughter"

A kiss goodnight, then to her room
But in the hall, she paused to look
And saw her Mother bow her head
As her shoulders drooped and shook

An aching heart consumed her
As the sun does to a vapor
So, she colored pictures in her room
As her teardrops stained the paper

Her visits with her Father
They were always bittersweet
She couldn't wait to see him
And his hugs were such a treat

But, the place he stayed was scary
With machines, and tubes, and lights
Strange sounds and people bustling
And everyone in white

Each time, before she left him
They'd do something she adored
Her Mom would take a photo
For her to pin up on her board

Then, she would pray for Daddy
While her Mother held her tight
And after each gave him a kiss
They'd head home through the night

Remember back when you were small?
A birthday's near to heaven
And quite a monumental thing
To go from six to seven

For Gabriella, it was hard
To anticipate tomorrow
Though her Mother tried her very best
Each smile was tinged with sorrow

That afternoon, there was no visit
Nor would there be again
They both sat back in her Father's chair
And in silence, thought of him

They sat until the clock struck twelve
The night, black as a starling
Her Mother softly whispered
"Happy birthday my sweet darling"

As Gabriella rubbed her eyes
From the chair, her Mom detached
And returned holding a present
Wrapped in pink, a bow that matched

"This gift is from your Daddy
He did all that he could do
He fought so hard for both of us
His last thoughts were filled with you"

"He wanted you to have this"
Her voice broke the slightest bit
"Your Daddy truly loved you
Go ahead and open it"

With care, she tore the paper
Set the bow beside the chair
Then soon, the box was opened
And all she could do was stare

Inside were shoes so beautiful
For a princess or a queen
As white as newly fallen snow
With stones that shone and gleamed

But, then she noticed something
That tempered the surprise
These shoes were not a little girl's
They were more her Mother's size

She held the box in puzzlement
"Now why would Daddy get me
Such beautiful, exquisite shoes
That clearly do not fit me?"

Then, searching further in the box
So carefully and hard
There, underneath the shoes she found
A happy birthday card

She removed it from the envelope
The words were so inviting
And here is what was written
In her Dad's distinctive writing

"My darling little Gabby
How I wish I could be there
To tell you happy birthday
Give you hugs, and smell your hair"

"I pray my words stay with you
Like a deep and glowing ember
And know, I'm never really gone
If you simply just remember"

"Every time you see a seashell
Take a walk along the shore
Take in a game of baseball
Hear the crowd stand-up and roar"

"And, when you're sitting quietly
Just coloring your art
Look up, and I'll be there
If you're looking with your heart"

"This brings me to your present
And I'm sure you're wondering why
The shoes, the gift I've given
You can't wear till time goes by"

"Someday you'll meet somebody
And you'll love like Mom and I
You'll never want to let him go
He'll take you as his bride"

"These shoes are for your wedding
And before the music's through
Just close your eyes and think of me
And I'll be there to dance with you"

As she finished reading
These treasured words from Dad
Mom sat down beside her
With a face more proud than sad

And, cuddled there together
In the chair so soft and deep
The card slipped from her fingers
As they both fell fast asleep

For, none of us can really know
The time that will be granted
In the end, all that endures
Are all the seeds of love we've planted

Life's souvenirs are memories
Store-up the ones you choose
And know, they wait to dance with you
Like Gabriella's shoes

DEVOTIONAL THOUGHTS

I love to poke around second-hand stores and estate sales. It's like a treasure hunt, and you never know what you will come across. But, in these trips I'm always struck by the thought that all these items were once someone's possessions. This gets especially poignant when you find collections, a gathering of specific items that someone may have spent a life-time putting together. At one time, they meant something special to that individual, and now here they are at Goodwill on sale for $ .99.

It makes me ask myself "what am I leaving behind?" And, I think the only meaningful answer to that question is the investment of love I make in those whom God has entrusted to me. There's a great song by Tim McGraw called "Live Like You Were Dying." Meaning, live as if you know your time here is not infinite and focus on the things that are really important. Let's live intentionally and fully and be willing to give life away to those who need it. Let's make that our legacy.

HONEST
HENRY'S STORE

What you build, build on the Rock

*Therefore, everyone who hears these words of mine and puts
them into practice is like a wise man who built his house on the rock.
The rain came down and the streams rose, and the winds blew and beat
against that house; yet it did not fall, because it had its foundation on
the rock. But everyone who hears these words of mine and does not put
them into practice is like a foolish man who built his house on sand.
The rain came down, the streams rose, and the winds blew and
beat against that house, and it fell with a great crash.*

MATTHEW 7:24-27 (NIV)

There's nothing like the morning
When a storm has finally passed
To see the sun now overcome
Dense, darkened clouds at last

Though all things now have a shadow
Wet dripping is still the sound
That we hear amidst the wreckage
Scattered plainly all around

It appears the ocean came ashore
Pushed landward by the wind
To cause distress and havoc
Then rolled out to sea again

It's left behind such chaos
And a mess beyond compare
Dead fish and muddy seaweed
Strewn about, just everywhere

There's hills of random ruin
Left tangled by the sea
And piles of boards and roofing tiles
Where buildings used to be

Afloat in pools of water
And half-buried in the sand
Are a plethora of items
That were once brand new and grand

Stools from a soda fountain
Lie upside-down and buried
The countertop is missing
Lord only knows where that's been carried

A sign that lists the flavors
Is resting in the moisture
All the syrup's in the water
Now enjoyed by clam and oyster

Down passed these wrecked confections
Lie shoes of every size
While suits and pants are floating
Alongside hats and shirts and ties

In the next intriguing pile
Where they've been transferred by the sea
Are violins and cellos
Black-and-white piano keys

Tubas, trumpets, saxophones
That once were played so gaily
Rest beside a Celtic flute
And Hawaiian ukulele

There's remnants of a barbershop
And a fifty-room hotel
Repetitious in their bobbing
Up-and-down on each new swell

Yet, amidst the ruination
In this devastated land
One building has survived
A single structure proudly stands

It's certainly been damaged
Where it sits beyond the quay
But, it's weathered nature's fury
And it wasn't washed away

Though the sign is cracked and twisted
It remains above the door
Where you still can see the letters
Reading "Honest Henry's Store"

For twenty-seven years
This place served this community
Established in the summer
Circa eighteen-seventy-three

T'was that year that Henry Parker
With his wife and baby son
Rolled his wagon down to Texas
To a place called Galveston

There, he searched for a location
To set up a little store
He finally found the perfect place
What he'd been longing for

With Galveston an island
Sand was all around the docks
But, through Henry's perseverance
He found a patch of firm bedrock

And here, he drove his pilings
To create a firm foundation
For he'd heard the Gulf of Mexico
Could bring great precipitation

When his store was finally finished
He wiped the sweat with his bandana
Then, gave the place the name he earned
Tending his store in Indiana

Honest Henry's reputation
Carried neither blot nor stain
And was impeccable for fairness
From Decatur to Fort Wayne

Though he built far-off of Main Street
His customers still found him
Shelves of canned good, tools and cloth
Filled the spaces all around him

The other merchants snickered
Laughing mean behind his back
"His location's so obscure
He built far-off the beaten track"

For they had all constructed
On much more appealing land
But, beneath their stores and businesses
Lay nothing more than sand

So, for years and then for decades
Through civil war and reconstruction
Proud Galveston expanded
Without pause or interruption

Honest Henry's stayed in business
Saw both prosperity and strife
Through these twenty-seven years
He'd raised his son, but lost his wife

Till at last, t'was time for Henry
With his boy now full-grown man
To retire to Indiana
And give his son the store and land

As they discussed the pending transfer
On the porch of hand-hewn oak
Henry's son sat down to listen
As his Father slowly spoke

"We've seen changes here in Galveston
And growth beyond my dreams
Many citizens are wealthy
So many ships of sail and steam"

"But, I've resisted the temptation
To raise a larger store and stock
For, there's no good land to build on
Beyond our patch of solid rock"

"You should keep this firm foundation
For my son," he said to him
"Just remember, on the Gulf
The storms aren't if, the storms are when"

He gave his son the key-ring
When the day for leaving came
Henry climbed aboard his wagon
To start his journey to Fort Wayne

And, as the Father left
The son (whose given name was Stan)
Stood smiling on the porch
And in his mind reviewed his plan

"My Father feared the hurricane
But they always veer far south
Or come ashore up north
More near the Mississippi's mouth"

"Galveston is sheltered
With a natural weather shield
There's no reason why I shouldn't
Exploit all that it will yield"

As he viewed the vacant holdings
To the east, and to the west
Stan said "Honest Henry's Store
Is going to launch a building fest!"

And, that's exactly what he did
He brought in lumber by the mountain
And held a ribbon cutting
For Honest Henry's Soda Fountain

To supply the clothing needs
Of wealthy patrons on the rise
Right next door, he built and opened
Honest Henry's Suits & Ties

There was Honest Henry's Barbershop
Honest Henry's Beauty Parlor
Honest Henry's Music Store was built
With speed and skill and ardor

At Honest Henry's Livery Stable
You could rent a horse and buggy
Honest Henry's Bath & Shower thrived
When it was hot and muggy

Honest Henry's Restaurant
Served quite exquisite pecan pie
And all the farmers bought their plows
From Honest Henry's Tool & Die

But, of all the building projects
Causing pride to puff and swell
Were the fifty lavish rooms
Of Honest Henry's Grand Hotel

Lest you think Stan disrespectful
That he thought Dad's way absurd
He did take steps, that to his mind
Honored Father's parting words

For, each time he'd start a project
It was well-and-widely known
That upon the sandy soil he'd place
A healthy layer of stones

Who could really blame him?
For this mix of stone and silt
Looked so much like the ground
On which his Father's store was built

But, looks can be deceiving
And no self-deluding thought
Can ever bridge the difference
Between sand and solid rock

As Stan was contemplating
Honest Henry's Pool & Park
The wind blew from the south
And then the sky grew thick and dark

The residents of Galveston
Closed shutters, sealed their doors
After all, weather had threatened them
So many times before

But today, it felt quite different
Something new was going down
As the wind assailed the sea
It pushed the Gulf into their town

The ships and docks and harbor
Were then violently consumed
Every business lining Main Street
Was reduced to utter ruin

The storm assailed the island
So relentless in its wrath
Heading straight for Honest Henry's
On it's wet, destructive path

It hit the soda fountain
And destruction took a minute
Honest Henry's Suits & Ties was gone
And all the clothing in it

The barber and the beauty shops
Succumbed to nature's power
Followed closely by the music store
And then the Bath & Shower

The restaurant, the tool & die
The livery all fell
And the hurricane just laughed
As it pulled down the Grand Hotel

And where, you ask, is Stan?
As wind and waves pound so erratic
He's in Honest Henry's Store
Crouched and frightened in the attic

When the hotel crashed around him
He'd looked on in pain and shock
Then remembered what his Father said
About houses built on rock

So, he dashed across the courtyard
Threw himself against the door
Where, at last, he huddled scared and wet
In the humble, little store

He'd kept it mostly for nostalgia
As a tribute to his Dad
Now, it was his final refuge
As his world grew dark and mad

He couldn't help but think of others
Those refined and rich and grand
Who'd built fortunes, lives and families
On a deceitful patch of sand

As the storm played out its fury
Taking many to the deep
T'was in grief and thankful sorrow
Stan, exhausted, fell asleep

So, we've traveled the full circle
To this wet, yet sunny morn
From here, in devastation
Seeds of truth can be reborn

Truth of your own foundation
What you're building on and in
And knowing when it comes to storms
It's never if, but when

Sand cannot be refurbished
Not by adding brick or block
It can't match the firm foundation
Given to you on the rock

What you do, do with intention
On the rock, and nothing more
And you'll endure to see the morning
Just like Honest Henry's Store

DEVOTIONAL THOUGHTS

We are all familiar with the storms of life. And, in the words of Honest Henry, the coming of those storms aren't a question of "if," but "when." Jesus didn't promise us a life without storms. Why? Because there is so much growth, maturing and learning gained in enduring a storm, that we simply can't acquire it in any other way. Testimonies are hard won. They don't come cheap and easy. Storms shape and build the power of our testimony when we anchor ourselves in the rock of our salvation. Once the storm has passed, our testimony gives us legitimacy and effectiveness when we encounter those who may be facing a similar storm.

Set your foundation deep in the rock. We may be damaged but we are not destroyed. We may be assaulted but we are not washed away. The rain will stop and the sun will rise. And we will be empowered to be an encouragement to others through our hard-won testimony of God's faithfulness.

EARL THE LONELY BEAVER

When God isn't finished with you

Is not wisdom found among the aged?
Does not long life bring understanding?

JOB 12:12 (NIV)

What a pretty, little woodland
Spreading out before our eyes
The trees dance in the wind
White, filmy clouds roll 'cross the sky

The hillside slopes so gently
To the quiet valley floor
Where sparkling brooks and streams run free
Till into ponds they pour

These pools of crystal water
They are here by grand design
Home to birds and frogs and fish
Oh, how they shimmer, and they shine

The author of this wetland world?
The master woodland weaver?
The builder of this sturdy dam?
Meet Earl the lonely beaver

As beavers go, he's fairly old
This is his fifteenth summer
With his wisdom and experience
He's the senior woodland plumber

He's sired and raised his family
Seen his children come and go
All with his wife named Florence
(But he always called her Flo)

He lost his precious Flo last fall
That thought still makes him wince
Without his wife or children
He's lived alone here ever since

Where once he laughed and splashed
It's barren, with his loved-ones gone
He mostly works upon the dam
Which makes and fills his pond

One day is like another
When you're a sad and lonely griever
Have you found you've ever felt like that?
Well, it's the same if you're a beaver

The summer task he works upon
The job that keeps him busy
Is cutting saplings for his dam
He chews until he's silly

He cuts each pole, and strips the leaves
Then works to drag it back
To place it high upon his pile
A quite impressive stack

It's far more wood than he can use
It's cut, it's stacked, it's dried
For, work's the only thing he has
To keep him occupied

And, when the day fades into night
At home, he's a lonely lodger
It's sad to think old Earl's become
Just another crotchety codger

Then, one morning he emerges
Climbing quickly from the lodge
For another day of cutting poles
And painful thoughts to dodge

He waddles to a likely tree
And quickly moves to chewing
But, this day's going to take a turn
For a little drama's brewing

He drags his latest sapling
To increase his inventory
And sees his pile is near half-gone
He exclaims, "Now what's the story!"

Someone's come and grabbed his poles
There's footprints in the clay
"I know my stack didn't suddenly
Grow legs and walk away!"

His anger brought his blood to boil
His temper hotly burned
He decided he would lay a trap
And await the thief's return

He settled in a hiding place
Where only eyeballs showed
How dare someone remove his poles!
How dare they steal his load!

His stealth was soon rewarded by
A noise beyond the bushes
He watched as through the plants and vines
A lone, young beaver pushes

The youngster walked up to the poles
And grabbed one with his paw
Earl sprang out from his hiding place
Shouting "Stop you thief!" "Ah ha!"

The little beaver froze in fear
At this angry apparition
He'd have likely died right then and there
If he'd had a heart condition

Earl was panting in his rage
He faced his thieving foe
"Move just one muscle my young friend
And we'll really have a go"

The boy, still scared and startled said
"Hey mister, what's the beef?"
"I'll tell you what's the beef," said Earl
"The beef is you're a thief!"

"You snuck here from another pond
And took my hard won wood
I don't know why I'm talking when
I should just thrash you good"

"It's your wood?" The young beaver said
"Oh gosh, I didn't know
My dad told me to gather poles
For his dam down below"

"I saw this wood and just assumed
It was open for the taking
I didn't mean to steal them
Honest mister, I'm not faking"

"Did you miss the marks of teeth?" said Earl
"They're as plain as a country mile
Did you think they just fell from the trees
Into this perfect pile?"

"I guess I wasn't thinking"
The boy said, through a cracking voice
"I was trying to obey my Father"
At these words his eyes grew moist

"I've tried so hard to please him
Ever since I was a pup
But, I never seem to make it
Never seem to measure up"

"So, when I saw this stack of poles
Towering right above me
I thought that if I brought them home
Perhaps... my Dad... would love me"

As he saw the youngster's anguish
Earl felt his anger ebb
For, the boy seemed sad and helpless
Like a fly in a spider's web

So, Earl's heart began to soften
That heart so dry and crusty
He asked the youngster, "What's your name?"
Through his tears, he choked out, "Rusty"

Earl said, "No real harm's been done
Past my needs this pile has grown"
"Help yourself," he winked and said
"We'll just call it a loan"

Rusty cried "You really mean it?"
Earl smiled and bobbed his head
Rusty grinned, then grabbed a pole
Towards home he quickly sped

Just as he reached the bushes
He stopped and did a spin
"Hey sir, would it be fine with you
If I visit you again?"

And, in that golden moment
Earl thought of his daughters and sons
He smiles and says, "Why sure young man"
Rusty grins, and off he runs

In the days and weeks and months to come
Rusty came to visit often
And with each trip, old Earl could feel
His cold heart melt and soften

He showed young Rusty how to dam
A creek to make a pond
Where to find the choicest stones
How to weave in sticks and fronds

Earl taught him how to make a lodge
And keep it warm and dry
How to know the changing seasons
Just by watching trees and sky

As Rusty gains the knowledge
That Earl so freely lends
They've become much more than neighbors
They've become the best of friends

Then one day, Earl had a visit
(By now, these were never a bother)
But, this time it wasn't Rusty
It was a visit from Rusty's Father

"I'm really glad to meet you"
Rusty's Dad pronounced to Earl
"I've meant to come for quite some time
Seems you're the source of wisdom's pearls"

"My son is just enamored
With your guidance and your teaching
I'm so impressed to see in him
New heights he has been reaching"

"The timing has been perfect
For your influence to enter
You've been much more than a friend to him
You've been an older, wiser mentor"

Earl was touched to hear these words
T'was such a nice surprise
But, he could sense there was something more
He saw pain behind those eyes

"You see, I've had a troubled time
Connecting with my son
I know I can be hard and tough
That's how my Dad got it done"

"But, sometimes I see in Rusty
He needs more than I'm capable of
Compassion…my approval
And most of all, unconditional love"

"As one father to another
I need someone to center me
I guess what I'm really asking is
As a dad, would you mentor me?"

Earl just smiled and nodded
Something new had just begun
He'd thought his days of usefulness
Were long over and done

Yet, here he'd found new meaning
A new truth he had been shown
When you invest in someone else's life
You just enrich your own

Well, it seems Earl's been adopted
As the months and years rolled by
He saw Rusty grow up straight and strong
The pride of his Father's eye

For, Earl and Rusty's Father
Are now both true believers
They know you get, when you freely give
They're pretty smart…for beavers

Earl loves his new persona
It's the best one in the world
For, he's no longer the lonely beaver
He now goes by Uncle Earl

DEVOTIONAL THOUGHTS

If there were ever two groups of people who needed each other in this world, it's the young and the old. What a resource of wisdom and experience are those who have earned the wrinkles of life. Whatever our age, there is always someone entering a stage of life behind us who could benefit from our experience, insights and advice. And, no matter how old we are, there will always be someone ahead of us plowing the rows of life who we can learn from. The joy of mentorship works both directions – giving and receiving.

In the same way a ship's captain seeks an experienced navigator to help direct them through uncertain waters, so it is wise for us to seek relationships with those who have navigated life before us. And, what an energizing affirmation of life it is for us to offer the blessing of mentorship to another.

So, seek to be mentored, and seek to be a mentor. By doing so, you'll experience the fullness of life the gift of mentorship brings.

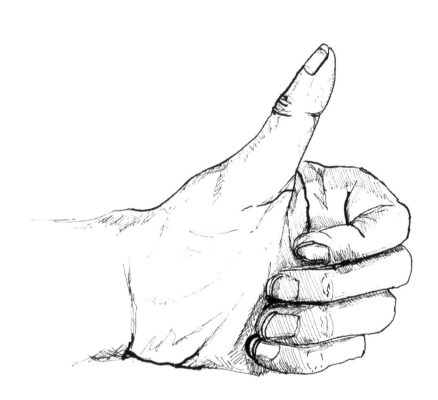

THE RULE OF THUMB

What happens when a member of the body calls it quits?

*But in fact, God has arranged the parts of the body, every one
of them, just as he wanted them to be. If they were all one part, where
would the body be? As it is, there are many parts, but one body.*

1 CORINTHIANS 12:18 (NIV)

Behold, the complex human body
    Some average, some chubby, some spare
    Some blessed with an hourglass figure
    While others are shaped like a pear

Legs may be gangly or knock-kneed
Like a cowboy, all bended and bowed
Faces are wrinkled with crow's feet
While feet can be called pigeon-toed

Hair may be bushy or absent
There's blue eyes, and brown, gray or green
Some body-parts take in the sunshine
While others stay clothed and unseen

There is cartilage and tendon and muscle
Nails, bone, tissue and scalp
Noses distinctively Roman
And those that belong in the Alps

But, no matter the characteristics
Of each individual part
They're designed to all function together
And never to function apart

But, what if there should be a rebellion?
What if design and synergy fail?
What if one little member refused to surrender
Well, there lies an interesting tale…

The thumb nursed a deep discontentment
His brooding speaks louder than words
He considers the other four fingers
To be shallow and vain and absurd

"Index just points or he scratches
And indicates he's number one
When twirled by the side of the temple
He calls people crazy or dumb"

"Ring is conceited and haughty
Sporting his bright golden band
For anything else he is useless
The spoiled rotten brat of the hand"

"Pinky, well don't get me started
Is there any as silly as he?
Acting all high and pretentious
When we're holding a hot cup of tea"

"Middle, he's nothing but trouble
Causes arguments, quarrels and havoc
Seems the only thing he's ever good for
Are gestures in rush-hour traffic"

"And, what of the countless expressions
That season our everyday speech
Is the hand only made up of fingers?
Why, if I were the mouth I would screech"

"There is finger-paint, finger-holds, fingerlings
Fingernails, finger-bowls, fingertips
Finger-sandwiches, sweet ladyfingers
Finger-pointing and yes, fingerprints"

"I'm tired of being second fiddle
I'm on strike till I'm seen as I should
Till I'm the one wagging or pointing
And chicken is thumb licking good!"

"I'll promptly suspend all hitchhiking
No thumbs-up for good, go or yup
Don't extend me to view a fine painting or two
And good luck picking anything up"

So with that, thumb resigned from the body
Just hung there, as limp as a fish
If this move was a cry for attention
Believe me, thumb soon got his wish

Hair went uncombed and was messy
Shoelaces, loose and untied
It was futile to zip up a zipper
No matter how hard it was tried

The talent to hook, snug or fasten
Button, snap, tie, clasp or cinch
Was suddenly slack and inactive
Along with a squeeze, pull or pinch

Thumb had now rendered a toothbrush
As useless as knife, fork and spoon
There was no folding a map, or tipping a cap
And forget blowing up a balloon

It was time for emergency measures
For the body to take up the question
Of what could be done to placate the thumb
And thus end this one-digit secession

There was surely no end of ideas
Put forward as options to do
The problem was, each body member
Saw things from their own point of view

The eyes recommended a movie
The feet said, "Let's go for a walk"
The nose thought the answer was flowers
The ears cried, "Beethoven or Bach!"

A massage was suggested by shoulders
The mouth called for anything sweet
The stomach endorsed that idea
"I agree, let's get something to eat"

The lungs thought fresh-air was in order
That was ok with the liver and spine
But, the hips and the knees, as quick as you please
Said, "That's out, as we don't want to climb"

The neck felt a keen twinge of tension
The nerves were beginning to fray
The body was ceasing to function
With the anatomy in disarray

Just when it seemed the whole system
Was headed for certain collapse
Another part spoke with distinction
"May I make a comment, perhaps?"

The talk was immediately silenced
To hear what was soon to impart
And all could detect the awe and respect
For this voice was the voice of the heart

"It seems that our brother is troubled
By a sense he's not honored or seen
He feels raw, and taken advantage
Just a cog in a thankless machine"

"We all know the truth in this matter
It's as plain as the nose on our face
We simply must offer each other
Appreciation and kindness and grace"

"Our friend, thumb, has shown us the issue
And I truly believe we should heed him
No flowers or movie or candy
Simply love him, and show that we need him"

"Besides, to be frank, clear and honest
And know that I speak from the heart
If we don't soon function together
We surely shall perish apart"

And with that, the whole body was silent
For, the truth they had heard, and they knew
Every member deserves recognition
No matter the job that they do

In fact, it would seem very likely
That the least, unassuming, the small
May be, in the Maker's designing
The most deserving of honor of all

They resolved to heed heart's admonitions
And voted to keep every word
But, before they could carry the motion
A humble pronouncement was heard

"I'm sorry, you guys, for the trouble
I know I've been selfish and rude
I didn't consider the body
I let ego and pride here intrude"

"I heard what the heart had to tell you
And I know every comment is true
I demanded respect and your honor
But I never gave it to you"

As thumb spoke to make restitution
Encouragement came from the heart
"I promise, I'll try and do better
If you'll just offer me a new start"

The whole body erupts in rejoicing
Celebration cannot be denied
The hands lifted in exaltation
As thumb goes along for the ride

The fingers and thumb reconciling
Is the highlighted part of the day
Again they are one, as the index and thumb
Make a circle, the sign for "ok"

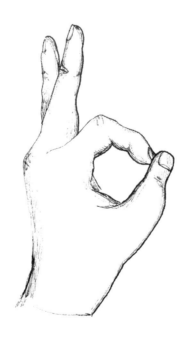

And later, there's washing and combing
Then, picking up spoon, fork and knife
They all eat a ravenous dinner
(Much to the stomach's delight)

With their unity cherished and strengthened
And with love and respect as the tether
They promise to not go asunder
For they know they're much stronger together

So, as peace settles over the body
And our quaint little tale now is done
The moral of the story? To God be the glory
May that be our own rule of thumb

DEVOTIONAL THOUGHTS

There is such freedom in finding our value and contentment in simply being who God created us to be. And in doing so, allowing ourselves to live fully into our role in the body of Christ. The Bible tells us we are "fearfully and wonderfully made" (Psalm 139:14). Not just as individuals, but also as people who He fits together with others to form a fully functioning body. So, can we honor God by doing our part, and celebrate and honor others who do their part? That's what I call body building!

PEPPER THE PRODIGAL CAT

A story of rebellion and redemption

But the father said to his servants, "Quick! Bring the best robe and put it on him. Put a ring on his finger and sandals on his feet. Bring the fatted calf and kill it. Let's have a feast and celebrate. For this son of mine was dead and is alive again; he was lost and is found." So, they began to celebrate..

LUKE 15:22-24 (NIV)

Walking down a sidewalk
On a bright suburban street
An early rain has caused us
To dodge puddles with our feet

We stroll past neighbor's houses
And enjoy our pleasant walk
When suddenly we see a sight
That makes us pause and baulk

Across the street, two houses up
There down upon all fours
A little girl is crying
In her half-ajar front door

I recall her name is Grayce
And she was dressed up like a queen
When she shouted, "Trick or treat!"
Outside our door last Halloween

But, she's not looking very royal
As she crouches there, poor Grayce
For, she's choking heavy sobs
And shining tears run down her face

We move a little closer
To see what she's starring at
And there, upon her lawn
Sits a bedraggled, skinny cat

Now, before I tell the saga
Of a girl and cat so gaunt
Remember, this story is fiction
We can do anything that we want

So, settle down and lend an ear
And hold on to your hat
As this narrative is told to us
By Pepper (He's the cat)

Hello, I go by Pepper
Gotta say, it's nice to meet cha'
Incidentally, my name
Is short for Pepperoni Pizza

I got that name from little Grayce
But her parents are to blame
"The first thing that she says," they cried
"Will be the kitty's name"

They sat down at the table
To enjoy a family dinner
Grayce saw and said her favorite food
And that name was the winner

I wasn't thrilled or happy
Not a name I would have chose
It could be worse, for her parents
Could have served her up Sloppy Joes!

All in all, it wasn't bad
Save for my funky name
There were lots of nice amenities
I sure could not complain

With a window sill for napping
Birds out in the yard to catch
A phony mouse to play with
Lots of furniture to scratch

I had a bowl of cat food
Got fresh water from a fixture
And, a litter box for when I…
Well, I think you get the picture

So, I settled into life
With this idyllic family unit
Then, they had to go do something
To absolutely ruin it

One day, the door was opened
In a second, just like that
It was worse than Armageddon
For they brought home another cat

I suppose he was adorable
He would purr and play with string
And rub against your ankle
If you like that sort of thing

He was friendly and obedient
Did clever tricks and stunts
In every way, the perfect cat
I hated him at once

Grayce had named him Shadow
And my temper got much shorter
He gets a really cool name
While I'm just a take-out order?

I determined then and there
And I avowed, I pledged, I swore
That I wouldn't take this laying down
Cry havoc! This is war!

So, I formed a little scheme
I would enact without delay
A subtle black-ops plan called
Operation Bombs Away

Wherever Shadow went
Seems he wasn't to be trusted
For in every room he occupied
Something...somehow...just got busted

In the bathroom, it was aftershave
In the den, a table lamp
In the kitchen, maple syrup
Got the floor sticky and damp

In the living room, a painting
In the hall, it was a mirror
In the library, the plaster busts
Of Tolstoy and Shakespeare

There was glass found on the sofa
Spots of perfume on the bedding
Off the mantle fell each photo
Shot at Uncle Larry's wedding

It was working to perfection
Soon old Shadow would be gone
Then, just when I tasted victory
Something suddenly went wrong

What caused it to unravel?
What short-circuited my plan?
Well, unbeknownst to me
They'd just installed a nanny-cam

Now, I'm the one in trouble
With "naught kitty" I've been tarred
While Shadow laps up bowls of milk
I'm exiled to the yard

I think I've been mistreated
Why, they couldn't be much meaner
Somewhere over the rainbow
I just know there's grass that's greener

I can find a better family
I can find a better kid
I can go and seek my fortune
And, that's exactly what I did

So, with sunshine on my shoulder
And the sidewalk 'neath my feet
Taking one last look behind
I set-off down the street

It didn't take me long
To find a likely new abode
Three kids were out and playing
As I stepped in off the road

One cried "It's a kitty!"
And they ran to where I stood
But the closer that they got
Showed me that this was just no good

They had sticky little fingers
Sticky shirts, and sticky britches
Sticky knees, and sticky faces
From their sticky jam sandwiches

Before I could escape
One picked me up, and held me near
Soon the jam was on my face
Across my paws and in my ears

I sought to flee the hugs
In which I found myself consumed
All at once, they shouted, "squirrel!"
I was dropped, and off they zoomed

The next stop in my search
Was with a family name of Tyler
It was working out until I met
Their ninety-pound Rottweiler

Then, I came to hitch a ride
With an old-woman in a Ford
She really seemed to like me
As she welcomed me aboard

We pulled into her driveway
And I thought "this could be heaven"
I had boldly rolled the dice
Would they finally come-up seven?

She brought me through the door
And to my shock, what do I find?
Her house is full of cats
I quickly counted seventy-nine!

I made a beeline for the street
I've no desire to be cat eighty
For the quintessential, feline hoarding
Neighborhood cat lady

After that, I wandered aimlessly
By tattoo shacks and bars
I had to dodge a motorcycle
I was splashed by passing cars

Spent a night curled in a drainpipe
Then, behind a place called Rocko's
I ate breakfast from a dumpster
Cast-off fries and moldy tacos

When it was cold, I shook and shivered
When it was hot, I'd pant and sweat
When it was dark, I'd hide and worry
When it rained, I got all wet

Till one day, a farming couple
Pulled up by me in their truck
She opened-up her door
And very kindly picked me up

We drove out to the country
Till we reached their little farm
But, instead of to the house
They took me straight out to the barn

"Here's your home now, lucky kitty
And you've got to earn your keep
You can sleep up in the hayloft
There are lots of mice to eat"

Did she say, go eat some mice?
I fear I've fallen in with loons!
The only cats that dine on rodents
Are in the movies and cartoons

It's becoming very clear
I may have overplayed my hand
All I've got to show are sleepless nights
And stains of sticky jam

I so miss my little family
Shedding on their shoes and sox
I miss my water, miss my food
I *really* miss my litter box

If I returned, would they forgive?
Would they be nice? Would they be hard?
They could exile me outside
And feed me scraps out in the yard

Setting out to seek my fortune
Has now made me come to see
That far from vile mistreatment
Few were fortunate as me

And, if they don't embrace me
If their greeting isn't warm
It's still better there than here
And eating mice out in this barn

So, I made good my escape
And left the farmer and his spouse
To find the way back to my
Little Grayce and little house

I will spare you all the details
How my homeward journey runs
Suffice it here to say
It's hard to hitchhike without thumbs

But, I somehow have arrived
And am now sitting on the lawn
Little Grayce opens the door
And quickly my concerns are gone

She plummets to her knees
As tears of joy she cannot check
Then, she rushes to the yard
And throws her arms around my neck

All this crying and the hugging
With her tears I'm fully doused
Then, she takes me in her arms
And we parade into the house

"Oh my kitty, how I've missed you
You're so skinny and so smelly
Your fur is stiff and sticky
What is that? Is that grape jelly?"

"Never mind, you must be starving
I'll get lots of food to eat
How about some macaroni?
Something salty? Something sweet?"

"Here, I found a bag of pretzels
And a jar of mayonnaise
How about a piece of cheesecake
With a caramel almond glaze?"

"We got doughnuts, we got crackers
We got cereal and cheese
We got broccoli, butter, biscuits
Artichokes, meatloaf and peas"

But, no matter what she offered
Carbohydrates, soy or fat
I just couldn't muster interest
After all, I'm still a cat

Then, she finally found an option
That brought teardrops to my eyes
She held out a can of tuna
Monster, massive, mega-size

When she put that in my bowl
And set it down on my behalf
She could not have pleased me more
If she'd served up the fatted calf

When I finished all the tuna
(And I didn't leave a speck)
She sprang one more surprise
A brand new collar for my neck

"So now kitty, as you wear it
May you always be reminded
That when it comes to love
It's here at home you'll always find it"

Well, it's nearly been two-weeks
Since my small odyssey was done
Yet, it really hasn't ended
Seems it's only just begun

Now, my mission's being thankful
Gratitude's my destination
My companions are contentment
Kindness and appreciation

I will never take for granted
What I had, and rudely spurned
And will cherish and remember
All the lessons I have learned

As I nap here on the sofa
Dreaming of my little Grayce
I'm startled by the breaking
Of a cut-lead-crystal vase

As I shake myself awake
And try to gather my dismay
From the hall I hear a voice
It's Shadow, calling *"bombs away!"*

DEVOTIONAL THOUGHTS

Obviously, Pepper the Prodigal Cat is a retelling of one of Jesus' most well-known parables - The Parable of the Prodigal Son. Jesus told this parable to illustrate God the Father's attitude toward His children who need to find their way back home from a sojourn of wandering and rebellion. But, how does a journey away from a loving Father start in the first place? The parable shows us.

Grumbling and discontentment are the twin sons of ingratitude. They can lead us into decisions that, in the short term, may make us feel like we are getting what we want. But, in the long-term, lead us to ever-worsening circumstances. A great rule of thumb is: The further we are from the Father, the further we are from joy and contentment.

If you are wandering, come-on home. There is a loving Father waiting for you. If you are home, remember to fight grumbling and discontentment with thanksgiving and praise to the one who loves you best. Pepper learned that lesson, and we can too.

ROYAL BLUE WITH STRIPES OF RED

God loves to use the small and insignificant

But God chose the foolish things of the world to shame the wise;
God chose the weak things of the world to shame the strong. He chose
the lowly things of this world and the despised things—and the things that
are not—to nullify the things that are, so no one may boast before him.

I CORINTHIANS 1:27-29 (NIV)

In a humble sewing room
  Among the pins and thread
  Lay a little piece of fabric
  Royal blue with stripes of red

It was a piece left over
From a project done in May
It fell outside the pattern
So was neatly cut away

Set aside now, and forgotten
It lay while pants and skirts
Were made in great profusion
Along with shorts and shirts

So, the dust began to settle
As the weeks went by and by
And this little piece of fabric
Could not catch the seamstress' eye

Then one day, the room was filled
With laughter and with light
The seamstress seemed so happy
Yes, her mood was sheer delight

As she settled down to work
Her machine was quickly humming
And soon a strap, and bag with flap
Was quickly up and coming

When her project seemed completed
One detail seemed to block it
She raised her head, "I know," she said
"It needs a little pocket"

She searched among her fabrics
Through the muted and the bright
Although she'd many options
Nothing struck her as just right

Was then, that something caught her eye
And as she turned her head
She spied the perfect piece of cloth
Royal blue with stripes of red

She set herself to sewing
And her needle swiftly played
Soon she stopped and smiled upon
The purse that she had made

And, in the special pocket
She gently tucked a note
She'd prayed softly as she'd penned it
And here is what she wrote

"This little purse is special
It's for a friend I'll never meet
Made with love, and filled with joy
For a girl who's young and sweet"

194

"So, I give it as an offering
As God would have me do
I close my eye, and see your face
For my dear, that friend is you"

Her purse was wrapped and readied
Then dropped into the mail
To begin a magic journey
And to start a brand new tale

For, after epic travel
And when finally it arrived
Caring hands prepared it
Placing special things inside

It's then, this gift is ready
Coming halfway 'round the world
To be placed into the waiting hands
Of a bright and lovely girl

She loved it from the very start
To her it's like a jewel
The contents help to keep her clean
And also stay in school

The thing she loves above all else
That makes her spirit float
Words from a friend she'll never meet
Written in a note

After reading for the hundredth time
The note and what it said
She tucks it in the pocket
Royal blue with stripes of red

DEVOTIONAL THOUGHTS

If there is one thing God has shown over-and-over again in scripture, it's that He specializes in the unlikely to bring about His purposes. There's David, the shepherd boy, defeating a mighty giant; the young nobody, Gideon, hiding in a wine press, leading Israel's armies to victory; Moses, the man with a speech impediment, becoming God's spokesperson to Pharaoh; and Mary, the humble teenager, chosen to be the birth-mother of the Messiah. Each is an example of God using the small and humble to accomplish great things through His power.

Royal Blue with Stripes of Red illustrates this principle beautifully through the Sew Powerful Purse program. Around the world, men and women use whatever material they have on hand to sew and donate beautiful purses to Sew Powerful. Sew Powerful sends thousands of these donated purses to Zambia, where they are filled with soap, clean underwear and reusable feminine hygiene pads that help keep girls in school during their period. This seems like such a small thing to us in America, but it's the small things that God will use to make big miracles. In the lives of these girls, it's often the difference between achieving success in school or falling into the cycle of poverty that affects millions of girls around the world. Each purse also contains a hand-written note letting the girls know how special they are and encouraging them in school and life.

Learn more at
www.sewpowerful.org

⸙ Acknowledgements & Thanks ⸙

To my family, Grace, Jared, Alyssa and Ivan. No man ever had better.

To Shonda Bowden, who beautifully puts on paper what I see in my head.

To Jason and Cinnamon Miles, great friends, great dreamers, great partners.

To Pastors Kevin LaRoche and Alex Ohlsen, constant sources of encouragement and friendship.

To Rich Stearns, for your kindness, and for showing me for 20 years what it means to be a Godly leader.

To Dr. Denny Frederick, you were just what I needed, when I needed it.

To Bruce DeRoos, the best designer in town. Here's to many more projects together.

⊰ About the Author ⊱

Dana Buck retired from the Christian humanitarian organization, World Vision, after a career of more than 38 years. He currently serves on the Board of Directors for Sew Powerful, a non-profit organization dedicated to helping children and families in Lusaka, Zambia. Dana has been a youth leader and mentor in his church, Renton Christian Center, Renton, WA, for over 20 years. He has been married to his wife, Grace, for 35 years. They have two grown children, Jared and Alyssa, and a son-in-law, Ivan. Dana lives in Renton, Washington.

Learn more, and inquire about speaking engagements at www. danabuck.com

⊰ About the Illustrator ⊱

Shonda L. Bowden has enjoying painting and drawing since age 7. She remembers watching Bob Ross on Public Television and being amazed at what he could do with paint and canvas. Shonda is primarily self-taught but has taken classes at the Art Students Leagues in Denver, CO, and enjoys workshops available in the Seattle area where she lives with her husband and two daughters. Shonda teaches wine & painting classes, as well as children's art camps in Tacoma, WA. She loves to use her skills and find new ways to express her creativity. She is inspired most by God's beautiful creation.

Audio versions of *Sew Powerful Parables* are available at
www.sewpowerful.org/parables

⁓ About Sew Powerful ⁓

At Sew Powerful, our mission is to combat extreme poverty in a very challenging place called Ngombe Compound in Lusaka, Zambia. We do this by equipping community members with training, tools, technical skills and jobs to make what we called "Purposeful Products." These products include school uniforms, reusable feminine hygiene pads & supplies, food and soap.

With a focus on the academic success of children, and the dignity of work for adults, Sew Powerful seeks solutions that are sustainable, and change lives. To learn more, visit us at www.sewpowerful.org

All proceeds from the sale of this book
go to support the work of Sew Powerful.

Made in the USA
Columbia, SC
24 April 2019